Great
63601

Contents

Acknowledgments

I would like to gratefully thank all of the photographers who have allowed their work to be reproduced: Rick Eborall, Steve Taylor, Mike Spencer, Matt Allen, Dennis Wilcock (who was also kind enough to assist with the invaluable archive of the late Bill Squires), Robin Stewart-Smith and the helpful staff of Milepost 92½. Of course, the many thousands of people who have forged and empowered the Great Central adventure over the last 42 years deserve due credit, for without them there would be no recollections to enjoy. Finally much love to Sarah, Agatha and George for their polite patience while I persist in following steam on steel rails.

TRAIN DEPARTURES

LOUGHBOROUGH

(CENTRAL)

15th SEPTEMBER 1952 until further notice

Time of departure — FOR

WEEKDAYS

SUNDAYS

Title page: **LOUGHBOROUGH** The Great Central has a strong working relationship with the National Railway Museum and often hosts working locomotives from the York collection. One of them is GCR Class 'O4' 2-8-0 No 63601, which returned to steam in 2000 and will celebrate its centenary in 2012. In its first life it was more used to hauling freight traffic; now it can often be found on prestige dining trains, as pictured here, when on 28 December 2005, with a light covering of snow on the ground, it blasts under Beeches Road heading towards Leicester. The bracket signal controls down trains approaching Loughborough from the south. Some components for it were recovered from Leicester Central station. *Rick Eborall*

First published in 2011

ISBN 978 1 85794 364 1

British Library Cataloguing in Publication Data
A catalogue record for this book is available from the British Library.

Printed and bound in Czech Republic

Silver Link Publishing Ltd
The Trundle
Ringstead Road
Great Addington
Kettering
Northants NN14 4BW

Tel/Fax: 01536 330588
email: sales@nostalgiacollection.com
Website: www.nostalgiacollection.com

Introduction

When was your first encounter with the Great Central Railway? My earliest memory of the railway is being hoisted aboard the footplate of the 'N2' for a cab ride to Rothley. This would have been in the mid-1970s. The five-year-old me remembers the jet-black LNER livery, being told not to put my fingers where they might get trapped, and calling out to the driver what stations we might reach next. On the way back I was offered a can of something fizzy from the buffet car and the whole thing was recorded for the local paper.

A few years later (I was probably eight or nine), Dad was hoisting me over the parapets of the Great Central Road bridge in Loughborough – not with the intention of throwing me over – but rather to see the Stirling 'Single' run through the station. No doubt your first encounter will have been no less evocative. Many hundreds of thousands

Nr. BELGRAVE & BIRSTALL A classic GCR scene, not too many years from closure. A grimy 9F 2-10-0 No 92094 hauls a train of mineral wagons north past the golf course and into Belgrave and Birstall station. The date is the 9th of May 1964 and it is still possible on occasions to see a 9F on a 'Windcutter' at this spot, though today it would be standing in the platform of Leicester North station awaiting departure. *M.J. Stretton collection*

of lives have been touched by the GCR, either as an ever-evolving preservation centre or as a grand trunk route to London. I would so like to be in the latter camp – to stroll along the platforms at Nottingham Victoria, or to ride across the viaducts into the heart of Leicester, and rattle south across the birdcage bridge past Rugby. Sadly, I shall have to wait for a time machine to be constructed before I can fulfil that ambition. Fortunately today's GCR provides an excellent flavour of this last great Victorian enterprise. Such a wide variety of motive power has graced our Leicestershire metals in the last few years that it is hard to know where to start when selecting cherished recollections. Instead I have tried to take you on a journey along the line, through atmospheric stations and classic lineside locations.

I hope that, even if you are a regular visitor, this book will reveal something new, or at the very least nudge your memory down a line it hasn't ridden for a while. We are fortunate to be spoiled by an ever-changing scene, so it would be impossible to catalogue every magic moment from four decades of preservation. I am grateful to the photographers for allowing their work to be reproduced. Thanks to their efforts and enterprise we can look back and reflect on a choice handful. And so too can future generations. They will be the next guardians of the GCR legacy, and future supporters are undoubtedly thrilling to their first experience of the railway as you read these words. I hope you – and they – enjoy (some) of the story so far…

Opposite: **LOUGHBOROUGH** One of the two surviving LMS Fairburn 2-6-4 tanks, No 42085, made a visit to the Great Central Railway to have new side tanks fitted. It then ran on the line in late 2009. It is captured here, perfectly framed below the railway's entrance sign as it runs round its train. From the booking hall beneath the sign, visitors descend to the platform via a handsome stairway arcade. *Rick Eborall*

Right: **LOUGHBOROUGH** On 22 June 1973 footplate and brake-van rides are being provided at Loughborough Central station, with Robert Stephenson & Hawthorn locomotive No 39 (formerly of Gedling colliery in Nottinghamshire) as the motive power. The sign on the platform proclaims 'Footplate rides 5p – Free rides in Guards Van on production of Day Membership Ticket'. How times have changed! *From the collection of the late Bill Squires*

LOUGHBOROUGH A general impression of the size of Loughborough Central station. This early-morning shot dates from 2009 before work began to repair and restore the steel, glass and wood canopy to its as-built condition. The station opened in 1899 and is now Grade 2 listed. The GCR adopted an island layout for the stations on its extension to London to save the cost of having to construct two sets of buildings on separate platforms. It also meant that, should a growth in traffic demand it, relief lines could be added around the outside of each station. *Rick Eborall*

Cancels Handbill AD136

Train Service

Nottingham Arkwright Street and Rugby Central.

on and from 1 January 1968 the following service will operate.

					SO			SX
NOTTINGHAM Arkwright St.	dep.	07 50	08 22	12 27	13 55	16 17	17 34	18 52
EAST LEAKE	dep.	08 03	08 35	12 40	14 08	16 30	17 47	19 05
LOUGHBOROUGH Central	arr.	08 10	08 42	12 47	14 15	16 37	17 54	19 12
" "	dep.	08 11	08 43	12 48	14 16	16 38	17 55	19 13
LEICESTER Central	arr.	08 24	08 56	13 01	14 29	16 51	18 08	19 26
" "	dep.	08 26	08 58	13 03	14 31	16 53	18 10	19 28
ASHBY MAGNA	dep.	08 41	09 13	13 18	14 46	17 08	18 25	19 43
LUTTERWORTH	dep.	08 48	09 20	13 25	14 53	17 15	18 32	19 50
RUGBY Central	arr.	08 57	09 29	13 34	15 02	17 24	18 41	19 59

					SO			SX	
RUGBY Central	dep.	—	07 11	10 30	12 30	15 05	16 20	17 37	18 55
LUTTERWORTH	dep.	—	07 20	10 39	12 39	15 14	16 29	17 46	19 04
ASHBY MAGNA	dep.	—	07 28	10 47	12 47	15 22	16 37	17 54	19 12
LEICESTER Central	arr.	—	07 41	11 00	13 00	15 35	16 50	18 07	19 25
" "	dep.	07 10	07 43	11 02	13 05	15 37	16 55	18 12	19 30
LOUGHBOROUGH Central	arr.	07 21	07 54	11 13	13 16	15 48	17 06	18 23	19 41
" "	dep.	07 22	07 55	11 14	13 17	15 49	17 07	18 24	19 42
EAST LEAKE	dep.	07 30	08 03	11 22	13 25	15 57	17 15	18 32	19 50
NOTTINGHAM Arkwright St.	arr.	07 42	08 15	11 34	13 37	16 09	17 27	18 44	20 02

Notes: SO—Saturday only. SX—Saturdays excepted

This service will provide SECOND CLASS accommodation only.

Passengers will be able to obtain tickets, **between stations served by this Service only,** from the Guard in charge of the train.

Accommodation will be provided for the conveyance of cycles, perambulators, etc., accompanied by passengers, who will be responsible for the removal of these articles from the stations.

Unaccompanied traffic will not be conveyed.

Season tickets, **between stations served by the Service only,** will be issued at Nottingham Midland, Leicester London Road and Rugby Midland Stations.

From:	Notting-ham		East Leake		Lough-boro Cen.		Leicester Central		Ashby Magna		Lutter-worth		Rugby Central	
To:	S	R	S	R	S	R	S	R	S	R	S	R	S	R
Nottingham	–	–	2/6	3/9	3/9	5/-	6/3	7/6	8/9	11/-	9/9	13/6	11/9	16/-
East Leake	2/6	3/9	–	–	1/4	2/6	4/3	5/6	6/6	10/-	7/9	12/-	9/6	14/6
Loughboro Central	3/9	5/-	1/4	2/6	–	–	2/9	4/6	5/6	9/-	6/3	11/3	8/3	14/3
Leicester Central	6/3	7/6	4/3	5/6	2/9	4/6	–	–	2/9	4/9	4/-	6/3	5/6	9/-
Ashby Magna	8/9	11/-	6/6	10/-	5/6	9/-	2/9	4/9	–	–	1/2	2/3	3/-	5/6
Lutterworth	9/9	13/6	7/9	12/-	6/3	11/3	4/-	6/3	1/2	2/3	–	–	2/-	3/9
Rugby Central	11/9	16/-	9/6	14/6	8/3	14/3	5/6	9/-	3/-	5/6	2/-	3/9	–	–

The return fare quoted above is that for Cheap Day Return

London Midland Region

Issued by British Railways
Divisional Manager, Furlong House
Middle Furlong Road, Nottingham

AD136X BR 35000 December, 1967

GREAT CENTRAL RAILWAY

Passenger Timetable 1995

Trains between LOUGHBOROUGH CENTRAL and LEICESTER NORTH from 7th January 1995 until 19th November 1995.

Miles															
0	LOUGHBOROUGH CENTRAL	dep.	10 00	10 45		12 00	1 15	2 30	3 15	4 30	5 05		6 20	7 30	8 05
2¾	Quorn & Woodhouse	dep.	n/s	10 53		12 08	1 23	2 38	3 23	4 38	5 13		6 28	n/s	8 13
5½	Rothley	arr.	n/s	11 01		12 16	1 31	2 46	3 31	4 46	5 21		[illegible]	[illegible]	[illegible]
	Rothley	dep.	n/s	11 03		12 18	1 33	2 48	3 33	4 48	[illegible]		[illegible]	[illegible]	[illegible]
8	LEICESTER NORTH	arr.	10 22	11 12		12 27	1 42	2 57	3 42	4 57	5 35		6 45	8 15	8 51

Light refreshments are usually available at Loughborough Central Station every day and at other stations at weekends.

Miles															
0	LEICESTER NORTH	dep.	10 45	11 25		12 40	1 55	3 15	3 55	5 15	5 50		7 00	[illegible]	[illegible]
2½	Rothley	arr.	10 55	11 35		12 50	2 05	3 25	4 05	5 25	6 00		7 10	[illegible]	[illegible]
	Rothley	dep.	[illegible]	11 37		12 52	2 07	[illegible]	4 07	[illegible]	[illegible]		[illegible]	[illegible]	[illegible]
5¼	Quorn & Woodhouse	dep.	[illegible]	11 45		1 00	2 15	3 40	4 15	[illegible]	[illegible]		[illegible]	[illegible]	[illegible]
8	LOUGHBOROUGH CENTRAL	arr.	[illegible]	11 52		1 07	2 22	3 47	4 22	5 41	[illegible]		[illegible]	[illegible]	[illegible]

Above: **LOUGHBOROUGH** After dark, Loughborough Central becomes even more atmospheric. The overall roof and the unromantic scale of the buildings have seen it featured in many films including *Shadowlands*, *The Hours* and *The Secret Agent* – each time playing a different location! The 'signature' station clocks not only mark the time, but also point the way to the cut-through between the buildings from one platform face to the other. Here GWR 'Modified Hall' No 6990 *Witherslack Hall* stands in Platform 1 on 16 February 1996 during a specially arranged photographers' evening. *Robin Stewart-Smith*

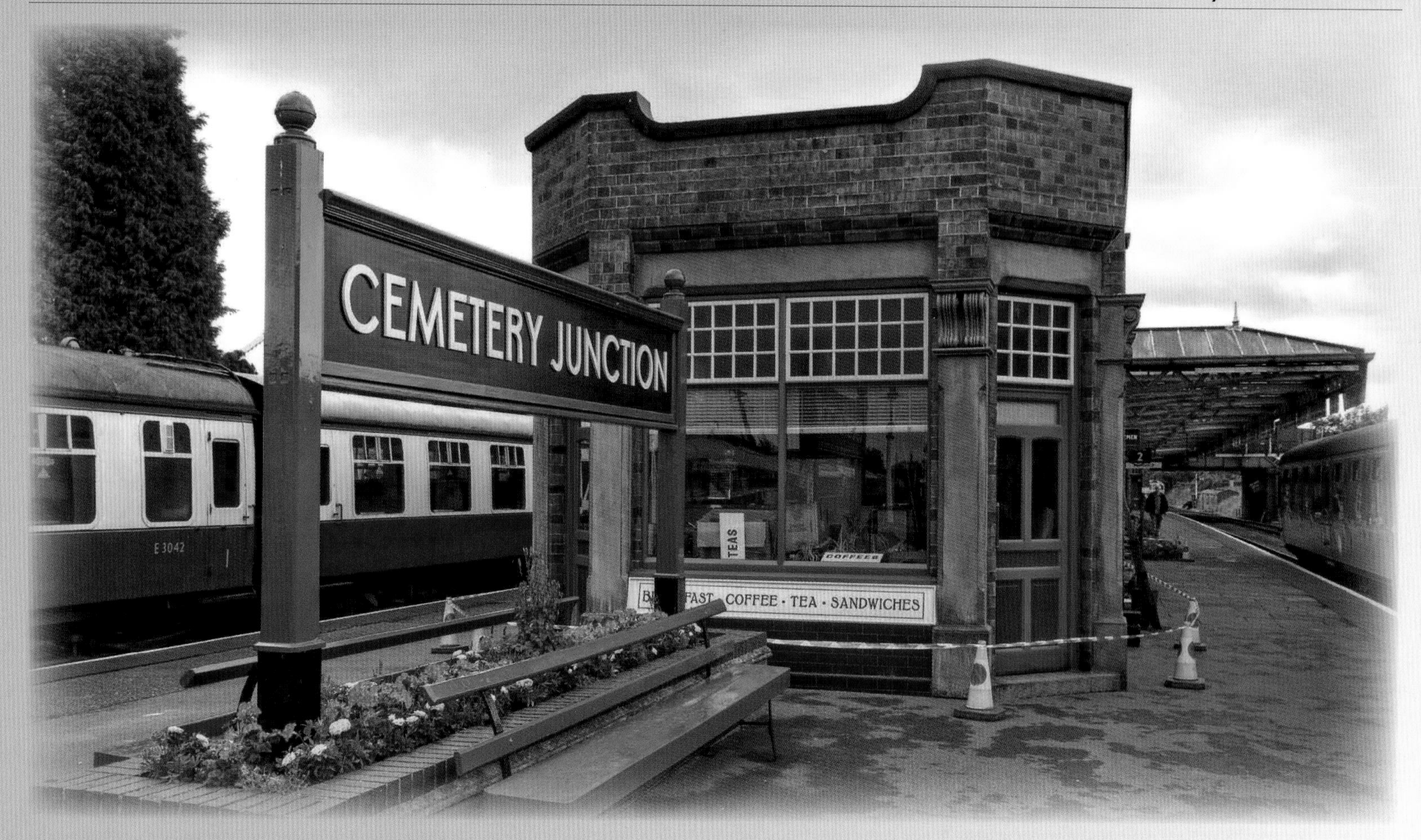

LOUGHBOROUGH Here's one building not in the original station plans! For the film *Cemetery Junction* (filmed in May 2009) not only was the station running-in board given a cosmetic disguise, but a whole extra block was added at the north end of the station. Carefully blended into the brickwork and the GCR architectural style, the whole thing is made out of wood, but this extra refreshment room looks like it might have been there since 1899. *Rick Eborall*

LOUGHBOROUGH Royalty meets Royalty. On 8 July 1985 Prince Richard, Duke of Gloucester, came face-to-face with the engine that bears his name. The unique BR Standard 8 4-6-2 No 71000 was in the last stages of restoration when the Duke (seen here in the light suit) came calling. Closest to the engine is the late Colin Rhodes, who was key to the preservation and restoration of the locomotive. Slightly behind the Duke is the late Bruce Lovatt; he and his son Richard devoted much of their lives to the rebirth of the Great Central Railway. The Duke's visit is being keenly followed by the media and we'll return to it later. *Dennis Wilcock*

Above: **LOUGHBOROUGH** Train departures and arrivals and a great deal of shunting at Loughborough are controlled from the signal box at the north end of the site. In February 2010 Signalman Chris Lambert is on shift. Above his head is the all-important track diagram, which indicates the area under his control, where the trains are and which lever relates to which point or signal. *Rick Eborall*

Opposite: **LOUGHBOROUGH** Another National Railway Museum locomotive – the sadly now retired LNER 'V2' 2-6-2 No 4771 *Green Arrow* – visited the GCR to undertake high-speed running-in trials in the spring of 2006. The GCR is limited to 25mph for passenger trains, but steam locomotives can be tested at up to 60mph in special circumstances. Here the 'V2' is hauling a passenger train out of Loughborough past an impressive array of sidings and main-line paraphernalia. The water column was installed to allow trains in the up loop to take water, but is currently disused. *Rick Eborall*

61994
65
A
EASTFIELD

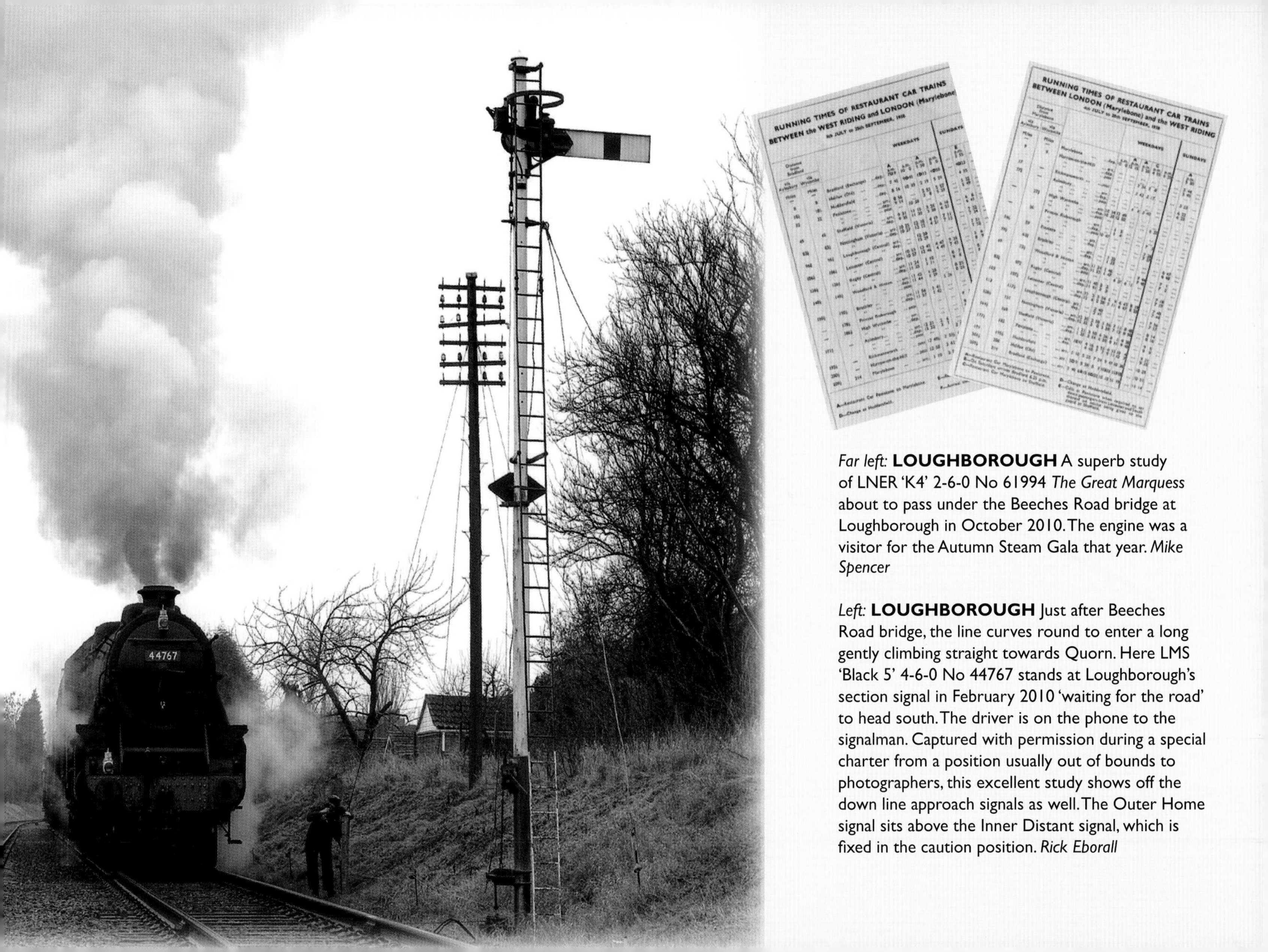

RUNNING TIMES OF RESTAURANT CAR TRAINS
BETWEEN the WEST RIDING and LONDON (Marylebone)

RUNNING TIMES OF RESTAURANT CAR TRAINS
BETWEEN LONDON (Marylebone) and the WEST RIDING

Far left: **LOUGHBOROUGH** A superb study of LNER 'K4' 2-6-0 No 61994 *The Great Marquess* about to pass under the Beeches Road bridge at Loughborough in October 2010. The engine was a visitor for the Autumn Steam Gala that year. *Mike Spencer*

Left: **LOUGHBOROUGH** Just after Beeches Road bridge, the line curves round to enter a long gently climbing straight towards Quorn. Here LMS 'Black 5' 4-6-0 No 44767 stands at Loughborough's section signal in February 2010 'waiting for the road' to head south. The driver is on the phone to the signalman. Captured with permission during a special charter from a position usually out of bounds to photographers, this excellent study shows off the down line approach signals as well. The Outer Home signal sits above the Inner Distant signal, which is fixed in the caution position. *Rick Eborall*

WOODTHORPE

Right: **WOODTHORPE** A study in greens: in the summer of 2005 the line's resident (former Class 101) railcar had been recently repainted, complete with a handsome set of 'whiskers'. Vehicle No 50321 leads No 51427 up the very moderate gradient towards Quorn. *Matt Allen*

Opposite bottom:
WOODTHORPE A wonderful shot from January 2009 of GCR 'O4' 2-8-0 No 63601, achieved by panning the camera to make it look as though it was at a high speed as opposed to the maximum line speed of 25mph. *Matt Allen*

Right:
WOODTHORPE
LNER 4-6-0 'B1s' were synonymous with the GCR route. Only two survive in preservation and here No 61264 in BR black livery passes milepost 94 with an appropriate wooden-bodied vehicle behind the tender. It is February 2002 and the new Loughborough ring road bridge will soon cut across the main line just to the south, changing the open view for ever. *Rick Eborall*

QUORN

Right: **QUORN** Finally – from somewhere to somewhere! On 24 June 1973 the Great Central Railway returned services to Quorn & Woodhouse station, some ten years after the station first closed. Passengers were finally able to join at one station and alight at another. In charge was Norwegian 2-6-0 No 377 *King Haakon VII*. The locomotive was a mainstay of services in the early days, having been imported with appropriate rolling stock. On arrival at Quorn, invited guests were treated to a clambake. The train is standing on the siding now used to transfer locomotives between low-loaders when they arrive and depart for gala visits. *From the collection of the late Bill Squires*

Tickets please!

Right: **QUORN** The harsh winters of the north in the 1960s are remembered in this cold scene from February 2009. A heavy snowfall gave the photographers on this special charter with LNER 'Q6' 0-8-0 No 63395 and the mineral wagons a rare treat. The train is arriving at Quorn, the lineside furniture completing the atmosphere. The mineral wagons were collected for the GCR following a special appeal in *Steam Railway* magazine. In the 1950s coal trains often took this route, their fast timings earning them the name 'Windcutters'. *Steve Taylor*

The platelayer.

Left: **QUORN** On a frosty morning in January 2004 three ground signals await the day's trains. This was the morning that the signal box at Quorn & Woodhouse was commissioned, giving extra flexibility to the double-track railway. This picture is looking south towards the station, and the signals apply to shunt moves from the down main (to the right). From left to right, when cleared the signals permit access to the road loading siding, the up platform, and the down platform. *Author's collection*

Opposite: **QUORN** Quorn station has some almost hidden delights. A former storage area under the stairs has been converted to become a 'demonstration' station master's office complete with wartime dressing. It can be found adjacent to the entry into the similarly themed buffet by the station roadbridge. *Rick Eborall*

LABELS FOR GOODS
A·R·P
VE-DAY!

Above: **QUORN** The up platform at Quorn & Woodhouse, complete with immaculate displays of wartime posters, awaits its next train in the summer of 2009. The majority of the country stations on the Great Central Railway's London Extension were provided with very reasonable passenger facilities, including a small canopy over the circulating area in front of the booking office. *Rick Eborall*

Opposite left: **QUORN** The National Railway Museum's replica of Stephenson's *Rocket* visited in May 2010 for a gala event. The open carriage was very popular – even in wet weather. During a sunny spell the vintage ensemble prepares to depart from Quorn. It will head north, using the crossover to reach the down line before making for Loughborough. *Mike Spencer*

Rght: **QUORN** Steam survivor, the unique BR Standard 8 4-6-2 No 71000 *Duke of Gloucester*, was initially restored at the Great Central Railway. The locomotive first entered traffic on the line in 1987, then became a star player on the national network. It returned to the GCR in late 2010 to take part in a gala event. It is captured here in beautiful autumn light on 17 October that year, leaving Quorn station and heading south – the open road ahead! *Mike Spencer*

Left and below: **QUORN** Immediately south of Quorn signal box the GCR is able to present a spectacle that disappeared from the national network in 1971. The award-winning Railway Vehicle Preservations Ltd has in its custody a unique collection of Travelling Post Office vehicles. Here the bags are being loaded for the 1937-built, Gresley wooden-bodied TPO carriages to make the pick-up. Look closely at the net in the second photograph and you can see they've also dropped off a couple of bags! These vehicles have now been retired for museum duties and are often on display at galas. Their place has been taken by four Mk 1 carriage-style vehicles, handsomely restored, which means that the non-stop mail drop continues to thrill those who come to see it. *Milepost 92½*

QUORN STRAIGHT

Left: **QUORN** Another look at that snowy photographers' charter train from February 2009 featuring LNER 'Q6' 0-8-0 No 63395 and the GCR's rake of mineral wagons. This time the train is captured ready to head south from Quorn. The driver and fireman look back for the guard's 'right away', the red of the signals stark against the snow. *Mike Spencer*

Below: **QUORN** South of Quorn the line runs dead straight. In January 2007 the railway was able to play host to Stanier 'Mogul' 2-6-0 No 42968 at its Winter Gala. The locomotive is at the head of the dining train set as it accelerates it train southwards along the Quorn straight. *Matt Allen*

KINCHLEY LANE CUTTING

Below: **KINCHLEY LANE CUTTING** The visit of BR Standard 8 4-6-2 No 71000 *Duke of Gloucester* in October 2010 coincided with the launch of the GCR's new Pullman dining train. The new train will complement the existing 1st Class dining train, offering exciting nights out with two large bar cars, and seating for 84. During the launch the new train cuts a dash into Kinchley Lane, the smart umber and cream livery perfectly matching the autumn colours. *Mike Spencer*

Opposite top: **KINCHLEY LANE CUTTING** Two main-line locomotives haul their freights in opposite directions. How often might this scene have occurred in everyday life when steam ruled the rails? Now it is the preserve of gala events or photographic charters such as this occasion in January 2007. LMS 8F 2-8-0 No 48305 takes the set of 16T mineral wagons north, while visiting LNWR 'Super D' 0-8-0 No 49395 is in charge of a southbound mixed freight. From a quiet lane which crosses the railway here on a blue brick bridge, the restored double track can be truly appreciated. *Matt Allen*

Right: **KINCHLEY LANE CUTTING** The same location is seen on a sunny spring day. 'Black 5' 4-6-0 No 44767 hauls a mixed freight south during the 1960s mixed traction gala in March 2010. 'Black 5s' were common motive power on the GC route in the final days of its first life. *Matt Allen*

Left: **KINCHLEY LANE CUTTING** Somehow, on gloomy days the pure main-line atmosphere feels even more real. Perhaps it is because the line was a workaday route, not a sunshine memory of seaside holidays. Stanier 2-6-0 'Mogul' No 42968 has visited the railway twice, most recently at the start of 2010 for a gala celebrating Lostock Hall motive power depot. In early February it took part in a photographers' special, and is pictured here leaving Kinchley Lane cutting heading south. *Rick Eborall*

SWITHLAND Viaduct

Right: **SWITHLAND VIADUCT** Flags flying, Norwegian 2-6-0 No 377 *King Haakon VII* leads the reopening to Rothley special across Swithland Viaduct on 6 September 1975. By now the locomotive was looking slightly incongruous – the Norwegian rolling stock that had arrived with it had been displaced on services by BR Mk I carriages (and even a Gresley buffet car further along the train). There was much-deserved ceremony in reaching Rothley again, though with British Rail demanding a monthly rent it wasn't long before the railway had to launch a share issue to buy the line and ensure that trains could continue to run at all. *From the collection of the late Bill Squires*

Left: **SWITHLAND VIADUCT** Golden low November light picks out BR Standard Class 2 2-6-0 No 78019 and its train as it heads north towards Loughborough across Swithland Viaduct in 2005. *Mike Spencer*

Right: **MOUNTSORREL BRANCH** The railway is lucky enough to be able to call on the skills of volunteers for all manner of projects. In May 2010, after two years of clearing vegetation and putting down ballast, a start was made on laying track on the Mountsorrel branch line. The line, a former route to a nearby quarry, was lifted in the 1950s and the entire length (just over a mile) is now being restored. The branch curves away to the east of the main line at Swithland Sidings. *Author's collection*

Right: **MOUNTSORREL BRANCH** This may be a book of recollections – but here's a glimpse of the future. Shortly after the Mountsorrel branch line point was installed at Swithland Sidings, several panels of track were laid (including a trap point to protect trains in the up loop from a runaway heading off the branch) and the branch exit signal was erected. To complete the picture three wagons have been restored in the livery of the quarry company that used the branch line. The restoration of the branch has been carried out by a group of dedicated volunteers who have achieved a huge amount in a short time. *Dennis Wilcock*

SWITHLAND SIDINGS The railway has an excellent selection of heritage diesel locomotives. BR Type 4 'Peak' No D123 powers north through Swithland Sidings with a Loughborough-bound train. When the railway was built a station was to be provided here, hence the gap between the up and down main lines to allow space for the platform, which was never built. Instead the station was located at Rothley. *Steve Taylor*

ROTHLEY

Below: **SWITHLAND SIDINGS** The sidings themselves were provided to handle the traffic from the Mountsorrel branch line, and here it would be marshalled into trains for onward dispatch along the main line. From the single-track line that survived after closure here, the scene has been recreated complete with signal box, up and down main lines, up and down loop lines and a phalanx of sidings. In May 2006 the railway's permanent way gang prepare a double slip for installation. *Author's collection*

Above: **ROTHLEY** Leaving Rothley and heading north, GWR 'Large Prairie' 2-6-2T No 4141 accelerates its four-coach train. As constructed, the ruling gradient of the GCR's London Extension was 1 in 176, making it relatively flat. However, there is a short climb both ways out of Rothley station, making for some spectacular departures. In this picture the train has crested the grade and it is now all downhill to Loughborough. The 'Large Prairie' resided at the railway from 2003 to 2009. This timeless study dates from July 2006. *Matt Allen*

Left: **ROTHLEY** Rothley has as many immaculately restored rooms as Quorn, only this time with an Edwardian theme. This is the waiting room, resplendent with gas light, original GCR mirror and a portrait of the (presumably recently) departed Queen Victoria. In winter a roaring fire always greets passengers. *Rick Eborall*

Below: **ROTHLEY** Rothley box (caught here early one Sunday morning in beautiful October sunlight) is an original Great Central structure, rescued from Blind Lane at Wembley. It originally controlled the junction from a four-track to a two-track section of the main line. Now it oversees the change from double to single track! The original box at Rothley stood another quarter of a mile further south. *Rick Eborall*

Below: **ROTHLEY** At the winter gala in January 2009 the Rothley signalman was kept busy with plenty of train movements. GCR 'O4' 2-8-0 No 63601 pulls into the down platform with the mail train in tow as viewed from the box. *Rick Eborall*

Below: **ROTHLEY** This trespass notice and bridge plate at Rothley are reproductions but complement the atmosphere of an Edwardian country station beautifully. *Rick Eborall*

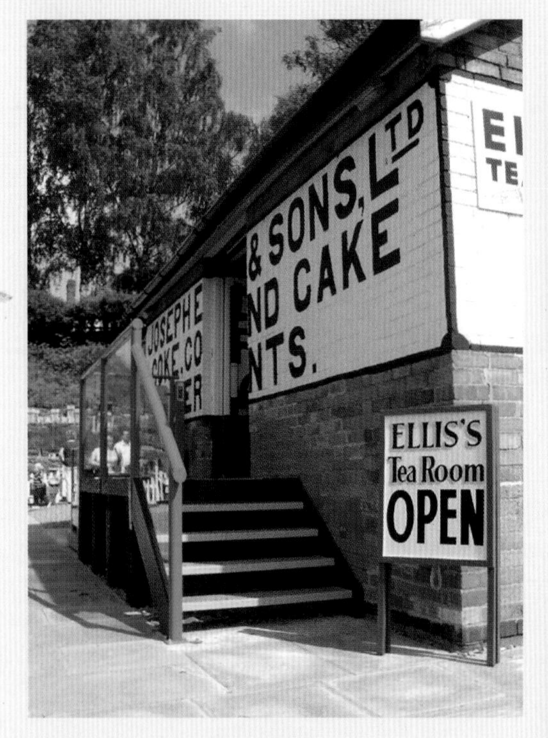

Above: **ROTHLEY** A former goods store at Rothley station has been carefully converted into an excellent tea room and makes an ideal place to watch the trains go past. 'Ellis's' takes its name from the company that built the store when the railway opened in 1899. As their carefully restored sign, painted right across the front of the building, says, they were 'corn coke and cake merchants'. Adjacent to the tea room is a very popular garden railway. *Author's collection*

ROTHLEY GWR 'City' Class 4-4-0 No 3440 *City of Truro* was a guest at the railway in late 2008. During the station's Edwardian Christmas Evening on 30 November that year, it pauses in the up platform with a dining train for Leicester. After dark Rothley's gas lights and the secluded location make for a very special atmosphere. *Mike Spencer*

Right **ROTHLEY** Leaving Rothley in November 2005, a train starts the climb out of the station, passing the tall starting signal and the carriage sheds on the left. *Mike Spencer*

Left: **ROTHLEY** Back to *Duke of Gloucester*'s visit. On 8 July 1985, having travelled with guests in a special train hauled by sole surviving GCR passenger express locomotive 'Improved Director' Class 4-4-0 No 506 *Butler-Henderson*, the Duke inserted a golden bolt into a fishplate just south of Rothley. This marked not only the start of works on the Birstall extension, but the start of fundraising for it! The track beyond the special train extended by only a few panels, and it was to be the end of the decade before passenger trains were regularly travelling south from Rothley. *Dennis Wilcock*

Nr ROTHLEY South of Rothley the line is single track, on the original down side of the formation (used by trains heading away from London). This is the view from the cab of 9F 2-10-0 No 92203 *Black Prince* as it heads towards Leicester. *Steve Taylor*

GREENGATE LANE The end of the line – for now. Work on the extension progressed rapidly. It was imperative for the railhead to reach a point south of where Leicester's outer ring road was proposed to cross the trackbed, otherwise it may have been permanently blocked. On 30 January 1988 a Class 127 DMU has brought volunteers and railway members on an inspection special. This is Greengate Lane, about a mile from the eventual terminus. *Dennis Wilcock*

LEICESTER North

Nr LEICESTER NORTH There is a foot crossing about three-quarters of a mile north of Leicester North station and BR Standard 2 2-6-0 No 78019 approaches it in beautiful light in November 2005. The trains here are on the down side of the formation. Restoration of double track to Leicester (effectively laying a brand-new up main) is a long-term ambition. *Mike Spencer*

Opposite: **LEICESTER NORTH (ON THE SITE OF BELGRAVE & BIRSTALL)** In the early days of preservation, before the line was purchased from British Rail, a number of unofficial outings took place along the full length of the line available. The track to Abbey Lane sidings – not too far north of Leicester Central station – was still intact. On one such working in June 1974 a train stands in the up platform of Belgrave & Birstall station. There is a definite flavour of the 'Titfield Thunderbolt' about the rolling stock, rather than a preserved main line. Three years later, the track here had been lifted by BR, the line was singled between Loughborough and Quorn, and the whole operation was barely clinging to life. A difficult decision was taken to demolish Belgrave & Birstall station; it was subject to constant vandalism and at the time there seemed little prospect of trains ever returning here. Happily, while the station has gone, you can still stand in this spot and watch a main-line train approach from the north, run under the bridge and into the new Leicester North station. *From the collection of the late Bill Squires*

BELGRAVE
& BIRSTALL

LEICESTER NORTH Demonstration freight trains do reach Leicester North occasionally. In October 2009 9F 2-10-0 No 92203 has arrived with the mineral wagons in tow. The locomotive is owned by artist David Shepherd, and its *Black Prince* nameplates have been removed for authenticity – it was not named in BR service. The basic run-round loop at Leicester can be seen here. Future developments will see another platform added on the right-hand side of this picture. *Steve Taylor*

LEICESTER NORTH
A busy scene at Leicester North station on 6 August 2009. GNR 'N2' 0-6-2T No 1744, itself freshly returned to traffic, has brought a trainload of VIPs from Loughborough for the official opening of the new station canopy. *Author's collection*
Far left:

LOUGHBOROUGH SHED and LOCOMOTIVES

LOUGHBOROUGH SHED
The early bird catches the worm at Loughborough Shed! Photographers can sometimes strike gold, with early morning light sending shafts through the shed as locomotives are prepared and move off for their day's work. Stanier 'Black 5' 4-6-0 No 45305 frames itself perfectly in its own smoke and steam. *Rick Eborall*

Left **LOUGHBOROUGH SHED**
The replica of 'Planet' Class 2-2-0 locomotive No 9, visiting from the Manchester Museum of Science & Industry, raises steam in front of Empress Road bridge as part of the Golden Oldies event in May 2010. *Mike Spencer*

Right: **LOUGHBOROUGH SHED** A dramatic long exposure captures GCR 'O4' 2-8-0 No 63601 at rest alongside GWR 'Large Prairie' 2-6-2 No 4141 on the shed apron after dark. *Steve Taylor*
Opposite page:

42085
48773
8F
48773

LOUGHBOROUGH SHED Pure atmosphere inside the shed, with LMS Fairburn 2-6-4 tank No 42085 and LMS 8F 2-8-0 No 48305 (posing as 48773 to take part in a special enthusiasts' gala event) in February 2009. *Mike Spencer*

Right: **LOUGHBOROUGH** A trip to the races on 10 or 11 August 1936 from Loughborough would have cost, in 'old money', just 1s 6d, unless of course you wanted to travel 1st Class at the princely sum of 2s 3d.

H. 1288

NOTTINGHAM RACES

TIMES OF RACING EACH DAY: FIRST RACE 2.0 P.M.; LAST RACE 4.30 P.M.

DAY EXCURSIONS

(Dean & Dawson's)

NOTTINGHAM

(VICTORIA) AND THE RACECOURSE STATION

MONDAY, 10th, and TUESDAY, 11th AUGUST

FROM		Times of Departure			Return Fares First Class	Return Fares Third Class
		a.m.	a.m.	A p.m.	s. d.	s. d.
Woodford and Hinton	...	11 25	...	...	9 0	6 0
Rugby (Central)	...	...	11 58	...	6 9	4 6
Leicester (Central)	...	...	...	12 30	3 9	2 6
Loughborough (Central)	...	p.m. 12 30	p.m. 12 57	12 45	2 3	1 6
Nottingham (Victoria) ...	arr.	12 48		1 4		
Nottingham (Racecourse)	"		1 22			

A—Through train to Nottingham Racecourse Station

RETURN ARRANGEMENTS

PASSENGERS RETURN THE SAME DAY ONLY AS UNDER:—

FROM NOTTINGHAM (Racecourse)	FROM NOTTINGHAM (Victoria)	FOR
p.m. 5 18	p.m. 5 25	Loughborough (Central) and Leicester (Central)
5 18	6 9	Rugby (Central) and Woodford and Hinton (change at Nottingham (Victoria))

In the event of the Races being postponed or abandoned these bookings will not operate, provided the Company receives notice at the station of departure in sufficient time to cancel the arrangements.

PASSENGERS ARE REQUESTED TO OBTAIN THEIR TICKETS IN ADVANCE

Tickets and bills can be obtained any time in advance at the Company's Booking Offices and Stations; also from the usual Agents.

Leicester Tickets may also be obtained from the undermentioned Stations:—

Belgrave and Birstall
Whetstone
Rothley
Humberstone

For further information apply to the District Manager, Victoria Station, Nottingham; or the Passenger Manager, Liverpool Street Station, London, E.C.2.

CONDITIONS OF ISSUE OF EXCURSION AND OTHER REDUCED FARE TICKETS

Excursion Tickets and Tickets at fares less than the ordinary fares are issued subject to the Notices and Conditions in the Company's current Time Tables.

Children under three years of age, Free; three years and under fourteen, Half-fares

For LUGGAGE ALLOWANCE, also see Time Tables

(O.T. and E.T.)

London, July, 1936. L·N·E·R 6,500

Printed in Great Britain by Knapp, Drewett & Sons Ltd., London and Kingston-on-Thames.—19746 R

Far right: **LOUGHBOROUGH SHED** New-build Peppercorn 'A1' 4-6-2 No 60163 *Tornado* masquerades as scrapped classmate No 60156 *Great Central* on the shed front in April 2010. Alongside is Gresley 'N2' tank 0-6-2 No 1744. This was an exclusive 'once only' photo shoot arranged in conjunction with the A1 Steam Locomotive Trust, which built the 'A1'. *Steve Taylor*

GREAT CENTRAL

TAIL LAMPS

Right: **LOUGHBOROUGH** Every Christmas Santa visits the railway, and for thousands of families a ride on the GCR Santa Specials has become a traditional part of the festive season. *Author's collection.*

Left: **ON THE FOOTPLATE** More than 8,000 people have experienced the thrill of driving a steam locomotive on the GCR. Here one of the railway's regular drivers gets to grips with Peppercorn 'A1' 4-6-2 No 60163 *Tornado*. *Steve Taylor*

Opposite page: **ROTHLEY** Visiting Riddles 'WD' 2-8-0 No 90733 pauses in the sidings at Rothley, while Duty Traffic Manager Alan Pakes consults the timetable for the next movement. Gala events at the Great Central Railway require many tens – if not hundreds – of people (often working behind the scenes) to bring ambitious recreations of a steam main line to life. This event in the autumn of 2009 was no exception. *Steve Taylor*

Below: **LOUGHBOROUGH SHED** Every good shed needs a cat. 'Mogus' prowled the pits and hunted around the huts north of Empress Road. A first-rate mouser and more than a match for pigeons nesting in the bridge girders, he could often be seen waiting for his breakfast outside the engineering mess room. Having retired from active service at the start of 2009 at the age of 21 he was sadly called away to patrol greater sheds than ours later that year. He is remembered in this official staff portrait! *Steve Taylor*

Left: **QUORN** Bright sunshine lights up a cold January morning, picking out the rails of the down main and refuge siding as a train heads south from Quorn & Woodhouse station. The steam providing heat to the carriages is blowing from between the last two carriages. *Author's collection*

Above and opposite page: **LOUGHBOROUGH** The past – and the future? The GCR has a long-held ambition to reconnect with another section of the former main-line route to London, which is immediately to the north of the locomotive sheds at Loughborough. Unfortunately the missing formation includes a number of challenges, including a new railway bridge over the tracks of the former Midland Railway main line. These before and 'after' images show where the bridge needs to go – and how it might appear one day. It's these sort of big ideas that continue to drive the modern-day GCR (in the words of the original company motto) 'Forward'! *Milepost 92½ and Great Central Railway collection*

156406

JOIN THE ADVENTURE – JOIN THE FRIENDS OF THE GREAT CENTRAL MAIN LINE

Do you come here often? Well you should be a Friend! Join the membership club that supports the GCR and some fantastic benefits can be yours. Generously discounted travel tickets are available for most of the year (except when advertised) including the big gala events. Keep up to date with the latest news with an award-winning colour magazine delivered to your door quarterly – and a news-sheet as well. There are also exclusive offers for Friends, and of course the chance to volunteer on the railway. If you become a first-class Friend you can also claim discounts on dining train tickets. Pick up a leaflet at any station or visit the GCR website to join a club that's going places.

Friends of the Great Central Main Line is proud to work with the David Clarke Railway Trust. The Trust is the official supporting charity of the Great Central Railway. Donations made by the public are used to advance projects on the GCR and promote an understanding of its historic importance. You can find more information about the DCRT and its grant aid to the GCR, and make a donation, all on the Great Central Railway website. www.gcrailway.co.uk

INDEX